ADDRESS BOOK

is for Avocet

A

A

A

A

A

is for Bullfinch

B

B

B

B

B

is for Coat Tit

C

C

C

C

C

is for Dipper

D

D

D

D

D

is for Eider

E

E

E

is for Fieldfare

F

F

F

F

F

is for Goldcrest

G

G

G

G

G

is for Hawfinch

H

H

H

H

H

is for Iceland Gull

is for Jackdaw

J

J

J

is for Kingfisher

K

K

K

K

K

is for Long Tailed Tit

L

L

L

L

L

is for Magpie

M

M

M

M

M

is for Nuthatch

N

N

N

N

is for Oystercatcher

is for Partridge

P

P

P

P

P

is for Quetzal

Q

Q

Q

is for Robin

R

R

R

R

R

is for Song Thrush

S

S

S

S

S

is for Tree Sparrow

T

T

T

T

T

is for Ural Owl

U

U

U

is for Venezuelan
Hummingbird

V

V

V

is for Waxwing

W

W

"Eggs"?!?

is for Yellowhammer

is for Zebra Finch

X
Y
Z

X
Y
Z

i like birds

I Like Birds is based in Moray, Scotland, and has spread
its wings far and wide to share its passion for
aerial wildlife and brilliant design.

ilikebirds.co.uk